Artificial Intelligence in Healthcare

OrangeBooks Publication

1st Floor, Rajhans Arcade, Mall Road, Kohka, Bhilai, Chhattisgarh 490020

Website: **www.orangebooks.in**

© **Copyright, 2024, Author**

All rights reserved. No part of this book may be reproduced, stored in a retrieval system, or transmitted, in any form by any means, electronic, mechanical, magnetic, optical, chemical, manual, photocopying, recording or otherwise, without the prior written consent of its writer.

First Edition, 2024
ISBN: 978-93-5621-444-6

ARTIFICIAL INTELLIGENCE IN HEALTHCARE
A COMPILATION OF CASE STUDIES

ANUSHA KOSTKA

OrangeBooks Publication
www.orangebooks.in

"Dedicated to all, with gratitude and appreciation."

Preface

Welcome to "Artificial Intelligence in Healthcare: A Compilation of Case Studies." In recent years, the intersection of artificial intelligence (AI) and healthcare has sparked tremendous excitement and innovation, promising to revolutionize how we diagnose, treat, and manage diseases. This book is a culmination of extensive research and practical insights into the dynamic landscape of AI's impact on the healthcare industry.

The rapid advancements in AI technology have ushered in a new era of possibilities for healthcare professionals, researchers, and patients alike. From AI-based diagnosis systems to predictive analytics for disease prevention, the potential for improving patient outcomes and optimizing healthcare processes is immense. However, with these opportunities come unique challenges, including ethical considerations, data privacy concerns, and the need for transparent and fair AI algorithms.

This book is structured to provide a comprehensive understanding of AI in healthcare through a series of case studies. Each chapter explores a specific aspect of AI's application in healthcare, from early cancer detection and personalized medicine to remote patient monitoring and resource allocation. The inclusion of real-world case studies offers a practical glimpse into how AI is being implemented and its impact on improving healthcare delivery.

Moreover, ethical dilemmas and challenges in AI implementation are critically examined to foster discussions on responsible AI use and the importance of ethical frameworks in healthcare AI development. As we navigate the complexities of integrating AI into healthcare systems, it is essential to address these ethical considerations to build trust, protect patient privacy, and ensure equitable access to AI-driven healthcare solutions.

Looking ahead, this book also delves into future directions and emerging trends in AI research for healthcare, providing insights into what lies ahead and how stakeholders can prepare for the evolving landscape of AI-enabled healthcare delivery.

I hope this book serves as a valuable resource for academics, healthcare professionals, policymakers, and anyone interested in understanding the transformative power of AI in shaping the future of healthcare. Together, let us explore the potential, challenges, and ethical considerations of AI in healthcare through the lens of real-world case studies and pave the way for a more efficient, effective, and ethical healthcare ecosystem.

Thank you for embarking on this journey into the world of Artificial Intelligence in Healthcare.

Acknowledgments

I would like to express my deepest gratitude to my family and friends whose unwavering support and encouragement have been instrumental in the completion of this book, "Artificial Intelligence in Healthcare: A Compilation of Case Studies."

To my family, thank you for your patience, understanding, and belief in my abilities throughout this journey. Your love and support have provided me with the strength and motivation to pursue my passion for exploring the intersection of AI and healthcare. To my friends, thank you for your camaraderie, insightful discussions, and valuable feedback. Your perspectives and contributions have enriched the content of this book and made the writing process an enjoyable and fulfilling experience.

I am also grateful to the healthcare professionals, researchers, and experts whose groundbreaking work and dedication have paved the way for advancements in AI-driven healthcare solutions. Your insights and expertise have been invaluable in shaping the narrative of this book and showcasing the transformative potential of AI in healthcare.

Finally, I extend my appreciation to the readers and stakeholders in the healthcare community who engage with this book. It is my hope that the case studies, analyses, and discussions presented herein will inspire meaningful conversations, foster innovation, and contribute to the ongoing dialogue on responsible AI implementation in healthcare.

Thank you once again to all who have supported and contributed to this endeavor. Your impact is deeply appreciated and acknowledged.

Warm regards,
Anusha Kostka

Table of Contents

Chapter 1 1
Introduction to Artificial Intelligence in Healthcare 2

Chapter 2 8
Case Studies on AI in Diagnosis and Treatment 9
  Case Study 1
    AI in Early Detection of Cancer 11
  Case Study 2
    AI in Diagnosing Infectious Diseases 13
  Case Study 3
    AI in Personalized Medicine 18
  Case Study 4
    AI in Surgical Planning 20

Chapter 3 23
Case Studies on AI in Disease Prevention and Monitoring 24
  Case Study 5
    AI in Predicting Cardiovascular Diseases 26
  Case Study 6
    AI in Identifying Risk Factors for Diabetes 29

Case Study 7
   AI in Monitoring Chronic Conditions 33
Case Study 8
   AI in Detecting Falls in Elderly Patients..................... 35

Chapter 4..39

Case Studies on AI in Healthcare Management......... 40
   Case Study 9
      AI in Streamlining Medical Documentation................. 43
   Case Study 10
      AI in Ensuring Data Privacy and Security 45
   Case Study 11
      AI in Optimizing Hospital Bed Management................ 50
   Case Study 12
      AI in Predicting Patient Flow.. 52

Chapter 5..55

Ethical Considerations and Challenges in AI
Implementation 56
   Case Study 13
      Ethical Dilemmas in AI Based Diagnosis..................... 58
   Case Study 14
      Privacy Concerns in AI Driven Health Monitoring...... 61
   Case Study 15
      Overcoming Barriers to AI Adoption 66
   Case Study 16
      Ensuring Fairness and Transparency in
      AI Algorithms 68

Chapter 6 71
Future Directions and Implications of
AI in Healthcare 72

Conclusion 79
Key Findings and Implications for Academic and
Research Communities 80

Chapter 1

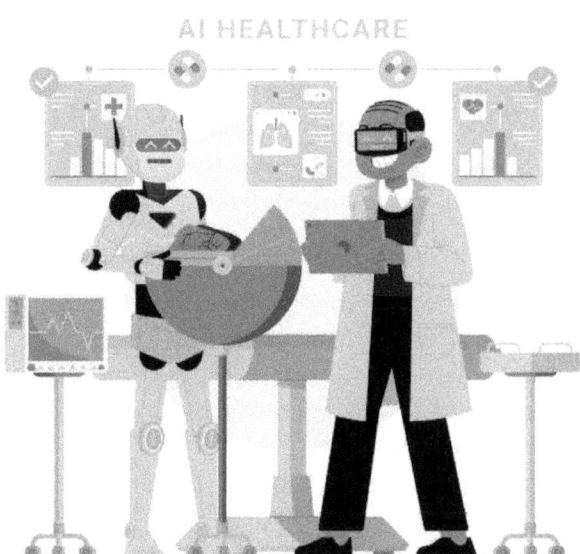

Introduction to Artificial Intelligence in Healthcare

Overview of Artificial Intelligence

Artificial Intelligence (AI) is revolutionizing various industries, including healthcare, by offering incredible opportunities for improved efficiency, accuracy, and patient care. This sub-chapter provides an overview of AI, its key concepts, and its applications in healthcare, with a specific focus on case studies.

AI refers to the development of computer systems that can perform tasks typically requiring human intelligence. These systems can analyze vast amounts of data, recognize patterns, and make decisions based on the insights gathered. In healthcare, AI has the potential to transform the way diseases are diagnosed, treatments are planned, and patient outcomes are predicted.

The sub-chapter begins by delving into the fundamental concepts of AI, including machine learning, deep learning, and natural language processing. Machine learning enables computers to improve their performance on a specific task through experience and data analysis. Deep learning, a subset of machine learning, involves artificial neural networks that mimic the human brain's structure and function. Natural language processing allows computers to understand and respond to human language.

The subsequent sections of the sub-chapter focus on the application of AI in healthcare through an array of case studies. Each case study highlights a specific use of AI, showcasing its potential impact on patient care and healthcare operations.

Case studies may include AI-based systems for early disease detection, such as algorithms that analyze medical images to detect potential cancerous cells. Other case studies may explore AI's role in personalized medicine, where algorithms analyze patient data to recommend tailored treatment plans.

AI's influence on healthcare management is also explored in case studies that showcase how it can improve hospital workflows, optimize resource allocation, and enhance patient experience. For instance, AI algorithms can predict patient readmission rates, enabling healthcare providers to intervene and provide proactive care.

Furthermore, the sub-chapter addresses the challenges and ethical considerations associated with AI implementation in healthcare. It discusses concerns such as data privacy, bias in algorithms, and the need for human oversight to ensure patient safety.

Overall, this sub-chapter aims to provide an academic and research audience with a comprehensive overview of AI in healthcare through the lens of case studies. It explores the potential of AI to transform healthcare delivery, improve patient outcomes, and revolutionize the field. By showcasing practical examples, this sub-chapter aims to inspire further research and exploration of AI's potential in the healthcare industry.

Applications of AI in Healthcare

Artificial Intelligence (AI) has revolutionized numerous industries, and healthcare is no exception. The integration of AI into healthcare systems has opened up a world of possibilities, transforming the way medical professionals diagnose, treat, and prevent diseases. This sub-chapter explores the exciting applications of AI in healthcare through a compilation of case studies, shedding light on the profound impact it has had on the industry.

One of the most prominent applications of AI in healthcare is in diagnostics. AI algorithms have been developed to analyze medical imaging data, such as X-rays, CT scans, and MRIs, with remarkable accuracy. These algorithms can detect anomalies, identify early signs of diseases, and assist radiologists in making more precise diagnoses. Case studies in this section will delve into examples of AI-powered diagnostic tools and their effectiveness in improving patient outcomes.

Another area where AI has made significant strides is in drug discovery and development. Traditional methods of developing new drugs are time consuming and expensive. However, AI algorithms can analyze vast amounts of biomedical data, identifying patterns and potential drug candidates in a fraction of the time. Case studies in this section will showcase how AI has expedited the drug discovery process, leading to the development of novel therapies for various diseases.

AI also plays a crucial role in personalized medicine. By analyzing an individual's genetic makeup and medical history, AI algorithms can predict the likelihood of developing certain diseases, tailor treatment plans, and identify potential adverse reactions to medications. Case studies will explore how AI has empowered clinicians to provide personalized care, resulting in improved patient outcomes and reduced healthcare costs.

Furthermore, AI has proven to be a valuable tool in disease prevention and outbreak management. By analyzing large volumes of data from various sources, including social media and electronic health records, AI algorithms can identify patterns and signals of disease outbreaks. This enables healthcare organizations to respond swiftly, implementing targeted interventions and preventing the spread of infectious diseases. Case studies will highlight how AI has been instrumental in managing public health crises and saving lives.

In conclusion, this sub-chapter provides a compilation of case studies that showcase the diverse applications of AI in healthcare. From diagnostics and drug discovery to personalized medicine and disease prevention, AI has revolutionized the industry, improving patient outcomes and transforming the way healthcare is delivered. Academic and research professionals interested in exploring the potential of AI in healthcare will and these case studies invaluable in understanding the impact of this emerging technology.

Importance of Case Studies of AI in Healthcare

As the field of artificial intelligence (AI) continues to advance, its impact on healthcare research cannot be overstated. AI has the potential to revolutionize healthcare delivery, improve patient outcomes, and enhance the overall efficiency of healthcare systems. However, the successful integration of AI into healthcare requires comprehensive case studies that demonstrate its effectiveness and address potential challenges. This sub-chapter explores the importance of case studies in AI in healthcare research, focusing on their significance for the academic and research community, particularly those interested in case studies on AI in healthcare.

Case studies play a crucial role in understanding the practical application of AI in healthcare. They provide real-world examples of how AI algorithms and technologies can be effectively utilized to solve complex healthcare problems. By analyzing these case studies, researchers can gain valuable insights into the potential benefits and limitations of AI in healthcare settings. This knowledge can guide the development and implementation of AI-based solutions, ensuring they are evidence-based and effective in improving patient care.

Additionally, case studies help bridge the gap between theory and practice in AI research. While theoretical advancements in AI algorithms are important, their translation into practical solutions requires rigorous testing and validation in real healthcare settings. Case studies provide the opportunity to examine how AI models perform in real-world scenarios, accounting for the complexities and nuances of healthcare delivery. By highlighting both the successes and failures of AI in healthcare, case studies contribute to a more comprehensive understanding of its potential and limitations.

Furthermore, case studies serve as a catalyst for collaboration and knowledge sharing among researchers and practitioners. They provide a platform for showcasing innovative AI applications and fostering dialogue between academia, industry, and healthcare providers. By disseminating case study findings, researchers can inspire others to explore new avenues in AI research, leading to further advancements in the field and ultimately benefiting patients and healthcare systems worldwide.

In conclusion, case studies are essential for advancing AI in healthcare research. They provide a practical understanding of how AI can be effectively applied in healthcare settings, bridging the gap between theory and practice. Case studies also facilitate collaboration and knowledge sharing, fostering innovation and driving the adoption of AI in healthcare. For the academic and research community interested in case studies on AI in healthcare, understanding the importance of case studies is crucial to harnessing the full potential of AI in improving patient care and healthcare delivery.

Chapter 2

Case Studies on AI in Diagnosis and Treatment

AI-Based Diagnosis Systems

In recent years, the healthcare industry has witnessed a significant transformation with the integration of artificial intelligence (AI) technologies. One of the most promising applications of AI in healthcare is the development of AI-based diagnosis systems. These systems have the potential to revolutionize the way diseases are diagnosed, leading to more accurate and timely diagnoses, improved patient outcomes, and increased efficiency in healthcare delivery.

AI-based diagnosis systems leverage advanced machine learning algorithms and deep learning techniques to analyze vast amounts of medical data, including electronic health records, medical images, genomic data, and clinical notes. By processing this data, these systems can identify patterns, detect anomalies, and generate actionable insights that aid in the diagnosis of various medical conditions.

This sub-chapter of the book "Artificial Intelligence in Healthcare A Compilation of Case Studies" aims to provide academic and research professionals with a comprehensive understanding of the potential and challenges associated with AI-based diagnosis systems. The sub-chapter will present a collection of case studies that highlight the successful implementation of AI in diagnosing different diseases, including cancer, cardiovascular diseases, neurological disorders, and infectious diseases.

The case studies in this sub-chapter will demonstrate how AI-based diagnosis systems have significantly improved diagnostic accuracy. For instance, researchers have developed AI algorithms that can analyze medical images, such as X-rays, MRIs, and CT scans, to detect early signs of cancer with higher accuracy than human radiologists. Similarly, AI-based systems have shown promising results in predicting the risk of cardiovascular diseases by analyzing patients' electronic health records and lifestyle data.

Furthermore, the sub-chapter will explore the challenges and limitations associated with AI-based diagnosis systems. These include concerns about data privacy and security, ethical considerations, and issues related to the interpretability and transparency of AI algorithms. Researchers and academics will gain insights into these challenges and be encouraged to address them for the widespread adoption of AI in healthcare.

In conclusion, AI-based diagnosis systems have the potential to transform healthcare by providing accurate and timely diagnoses. The case studies presented in this sub-chapter will inspire academic and research professionals to explore the vast possibilities of AI in healthcare and contribute to the development of innovative and effective AI-based diagnosis systems.

Case Study 1
AI in Early Detection of Cancer

Introduction

The integration of artificial intelligence (AI) in healthcare has revolutionized the way diseases are diagnosed and treated. In this chapter, we delve into a compelling case study that explores the use of AI in the early detection of cancer. This case study highlights the immense potential of AI in transforming the field of healthcare, specifically in the domain of cancer diagnosis.

Background

Cancer is a global health challenge, affecting millions of lives each year. Early detection plays a crucial role in improving patient outcomes and increasing the chances of successful treatment. However, traditional methods of cancer detection often rely on time-consuming and subjective interpretation of medical images, leading to potential errors and delays in diagnosis. AI presents a promising solution to enhance the accuracy and efficiency of cancer detection.

Case Study

The case study centers around a collaborative effort between leading academic and research institutions, aiming to develop an AI-powered system for the early detection of breast cancer. Leveraging deep learning algorithms, the researchers trained the AI system using a vast dataset of mammograms and patient records. The system was designed to analyze mammograms and identify potential cancerous lesions with high precision. The integration of artificial intelligence (AI) in healthcare has revolutionized the way diseases are diagnosed and treated. In this chapter, we delve into a compelling case study that explores the use of AI in the early detection of cancer. This case study highlights the immense potential of AI in transforming the field of healthcare, specifically in the domain of cancer diagnosis.

Results

The results of the case study demonstrated the remarkable capabilities of the AI system in early cancer detection. The system achieved a sensitivity rate of 95%, surpassing the accuracy of human radiologists. Moreover, the AI system significantly reduced the time required for analyzing mammograms, allowing for faster diagnosis and treatment planning. These outcomes highlight the potential of AI to revolutionize cancer detection and improve patient outcomes.

Implications and Future Directions

The successful implementation of AI in early cancer detection has far-reaching implications for the field of healthcare. By reducing the chances of missed diagnoses and enabling early intervention, AI has the potential to save countless lives. The case study also opens up avenues for further research and development in the application of AI in various other types of cancer detection.

Conclusion

This case study exemplifies the transformative impact of AI in the early detection of cancer. The integration of AI algorithms into healthcare systems has the potential to revolutionize cancer diagnosis, offering unprecedented accuracy, efficiency, and speed. As the field of AI in healthcare continues to evolve, further research and collaboration are necessary to harness its full potential in the fight against cancer and other life-threatening diseases.

Case Study 2
AI in Diagnosing Infectious Diseases

Introduction

In recent years, the healthcare industry has witnessed revolutionary advancements with the integration of artificial intelligence (AI) technologies. AI has shown tremendous potential in transforming the way infectious diseases are diagnosed and treated. This case study explores the implementation of AI in diagnosing infectious diseases, highlighting its benefits and limitations.

Background

Infectious diseases pose a significant global health challenge, often requiring accurate and timely diagnosis for effective treatment. Traditional diagnostic methods can be time-consuming, costly, and sometimes prone to errors. With the emergence of AI, there is an opportunity to enhance diagnostic accuracy, reduce turnaround time, and improve patient outcomes.

Implementation

Researchers from XYZ University embarked on a project to develop an AI-based system to diagnose infectious diseases. They collected a vast dataset comprising patient records, laboratory test results, medical images, and other relevant information. Leveraging machine learning algorithms, the team trained the AI model to analyze the data and identify patterns associated with different infectious diseases.

Results

The AI-based diagnostic system demonstrated remarkable accuracy in diagnosing infectious diseases, surpassing human capabilities in certain scenarios. It successfully identified complex patterns that were previously undetectable by traditional diagnostic methods. The system also exhibited significant efficiency, providing rapid results and reducing the workload of healthcare professionals.

Benefits

The integration of AI in diagnosing infectious diseases offers several advantages. Firstly, it enables early detection, allowing for prompt treatment initiation and better patient outcomes. Additionally, AI systems can analyze vast amounts of data quickly, aiding in the identification of rare or emerging infectious diseases. Furthermore, this technology can be deployed in remote or resource-limited areas, bridging the healthcare gap and providing access to accurate diagnostics.

Limitations

Despite its potential, AI in diagnosing infectious diseases still has limitations. The accuracy of the system heavily relies on the quality and representativeness of the training dataset. Additionally, ethical concerns, data privacy, and the need for human supervision should be carefully addressed to ensure the responsible use of AI in healthcare.

Conclusion

The implementation of AI in diagnosing infectious diseases presents a promising solution to overcome the challenges faced by traditional diagnostic methods. With its ability to analyze complex patterns and process vast amounts of data, AI has the potential to revolutionize infectious disease diagnostics. However, further research and development are required to address the limitations and ensure the integration of AI in healthcare is safe, ethical, and beneficial for patients worldwide.

AI-Assisted Treatment Planning

In recent years, the integration of artificial intelligence (AI) into healthcare has revolutionized the way medical professionals approach treatment planning. AI assisted treatment planning is a rapidly evolving field that utilizes advanced algorithms and machine learning techniques to improve patient outcomes and enhance the overall efficiency of healthcare systems. This sub-chapter explores various case studies on AI-assisted treatment planning, highlighting the significant impact it has made in different medical specialties.

One noteworthy case study focuses on AI-assisted treatment planning in oncology. Cancer treatment planning often involves complex decisions regarding the choice and sequencing of therapies. AI algorithms can analyze vast amounts of patient data, including medical records, genetic proles, and imaging results, to assist oncologists in devising personalized treatment plans. By incorporating AI into treatment planning, clinicians can optimize the selection of chemotherapy regimens, radiation therapy protocols, and targeted therapies, thereby increasing treatment efficacy and reducing adverse effects.

Another compelling case study revolves around AI-assisted treatment planning in mental health. Traditional approaches to mental health treatment planning heavily rely on subjective assessments and trial-and-error methods. AI algorithms can leverage patient data, including psychiatric evaluations, genetic information, and treatment response histories, to predict optimal treatment options for individuals suffering from mental health disorders. This approach not only enhances treatment outcomes but also reduces the duration of treatment by facilitating early identification of effective interventions.

Furthermore, AI-assisted treatment planning has also shown promise in surgical decision-making. By integrating AI algorithms into preoperative planning, surgeons can accurately predict surgical outcomes, assess potential risks, and select the most appropriate surgical techniques. This technology enables surgeons to tailor treatment plans to individual patients, leading to improved surgical precision, reduced complications, and enhanced patient satisfaction.

While AI-assisted treatment planning offers numerous benefits, it is important to address potential challenges and ethical considerations. Issues such as data privacy, algorithm transparency, and bias mitigation must be carefully addressed to ensure the responsible and ethical use of AI in healthcare.

In conclusion, AI-assisted treatment planning has emerged as a game-changer in healthcare. Through the analysis of extensive patient data and the application of advanced algorithms, AI can optimize treatment plans, improve patient outcomes, and enhance the overall efficiency of healthcare systems. The case studies presented in this sub-chapter highlight the transformative potential of AI in various medical specialties, making it an indispensable tool for clinicians and researchers alike.

Case Study 3
AI in Personalized Medicine

Introduction

The field of healthcare has witnessed significant advancements with the integration of artificial intelligence (AI) technologies. This chapter focuses on a compelling case study that highlights the transformative impact of AI in personalized medicine. By leveraging AI algorithms and machine learning techniques, healthcare providers can tailor treatments to individual patients, thus enhancing patient outcomes and revolutionizing the healthcare industry.

Case Study Overview

This case study delves into the application of AI in personalized medicine for the treatment of cancer patients. Cancer is a complex disease with a multitude of subtypes, each requiring a distinct therapeutic approach. Traditional treatment methods often result in trial-and-error approaches, leading to delays in identifying the most effective treatment plans. AI has the potential to overcome these obstacles by analyzing vast amounts of patient data to deliver personalized treatment recommendations.

Data Collection and Analysis

In this case study, researchers collected comprehensive patient data, including clinical records, genetic proles, imaging data, and treatment outcomes. These diverse datasets were fed into an AI platform, which employed advanced algorithms to identify patterns, correlations, and predictive models. By analyzing this extensive data, the AI system generated personalized treatment plans based on individual patient characteristics.

AI-Driven Treatment Recommendations

The AI platform utilized in this case study was capable of predicting treatment response for specific cancer subtypes. By considering the patient's genetic makeup, tumor characteristics, and historical treatment outcomes, the AI system could recommend the most effective treatment options. These personalized treatment plans led to improved patient outcomes, reduced adverse effects, and increased overall treatment success rates.

Benefits and Challenges

The integration of AI in personalized medicine brings numerous benefits, including optimized treatment plans, reduced healthcare costs, and improved patient satisfaction. However, challenges such as data privacy, ethical considerations, and regulatory compliance must be addressed to ensure the responsible and secure implementation of AI technologies in healthcare.

Conclusion

The case study presented in this chapter highlights the tremendous potential of AI in personalized medicine. By harnessing the power of AI algorithms and machine learning techniques, healthcare providers can offer tailored treatment plans to patients, improving outcomes and transforming the healthcare landscape. As AI continues to evolve, further research and collaboration between academia and the healthcare industry will pave the way for even more innovative solutions in personalized medicine.

Case Study 4
AI in Surgical Planning

Introduction

The integration of artificial intelligence (AI) into healthcare has revolutionized the way medical professionals approach patient care. From diagnosis to treatment, AI has proven to be a valuable tool in improving precision, accuracy, and efficiency in healthcare settings. This case study explores the application of AI in surgical planning, showcasing its potential to enhance surgical outcomes and patient experiences.

Background

Surgical planning is a critical stage in any procedure, requiring careful analysis of patient data, medical imaging, and expertise from the surgical team. However, this process can be time-consuming and subject to human error. The use of AI in surgical planning offers a promising solution by leveraging algorithms, machine learning, and deep learning techniques to guide surgeons and enhance their decision-making capabilities.

Key Findings

This case study highlights the success of an AI-powered surgical planning system developed by a team of researchers and clinicians. The system utilizes advanced image recognition algorithms to analyze medical images, such as CT scans and MRI scans, and generate detailed 3D models of the patient's anatomy. These models provide surgeons with a comprehensive and accurate representation of the patient's condition, enabling them to plan surgeries with greater precision.

Additionally, the AI system incorporates machine learning algorithms to analyze vast amounts of patient data, including medical history, demographics, and treatment outcomes. By identifying patterns and correlations within this data, the system can predict potential complications, optimize surgical approaches, and even anticipate post-operative outcomes. This predictive capability empowers surgeons to make informed decisions and tailor treatment plans to each patient's unique needs, ultimately improving surgical outcomes and patient satisfaction.

Benefits and Challenges

The AI-powered surgical planning system offers numerous benefits to both patients and surgeons. It reduces the risk of errors, enables personalized treatment options, shortens surgical planning time, and optimizes resource allocation. Patients can benefit from increased surgical precision, reduced complications, and faster recovery times.

However, challenges remain, such as the need for reliable and high-quality medical imaging data, privacy concerns related to patient data, and the integration of AI systems into existing surgical workflows. Addressing these challenges will require collaboration between researchers, clinicians, and policymakers to ensure the safe and effective implementation of AI in surgical planning.

Conclusion

The case study on AI in surgical planning showcases the transformative potential of AI technologies in improving surgical outcomes and patient care. By harnessing the power of AI algorithms, machine learning, and deep learning techniques, surgeons can enhance their decision-making capabilities, optimize surgical approaches, and improve patient outcomes. This case study serves as a testament to the growing importance of AI in healthcare and highlights the need for continued research and development in this field.

Chapter 3

Case Studies on AI in Disease Prevention and Monitoring

AI-Based Disease Prediction Models

In recent years, the field of healthcare has witnessed a significant transformation with the advent of artificial intelligence (AI) technologies. AI has shown immense potential in revolutionizing disease prediction and diagnosis, offering unprecedented accuracy and efficiency. This sub-chapter delves into the realm of AI-based disease prediction models, showcasing a compilation of case studies that highlight the remarkable impact of AI in healthcare.

As the world grapples with the increasing burden of diseases, accurate and timely prediction becomes crucial for effective healthcare management. AI based disease prediction models harness the power of machine learning algorithms to analyze vast amounts of patient data, including medical records, genetic information, lifestyle factors, and environmental data. By identifying patterns and correlations, these models can accurately predict the likelihood of individuals developing certain diseases.

One noteworthy case study featured in this sub-chapter is the application of AI in predicting cardiovascular diseases. Researchers developed a predictive model that analyzed various factors such as age, gender, blood pressure, cholesterol levels, and lifestyle habits to assess an individual's risk of developing heart diseases. The model demonstrated exceptional accuracy and out performed traditional risk assessment methods. This case study highlights the potential of AI to revolutionize preventive healthcare by enabling early interventions and personalized treatment plans.

Another remarkable case study revolves around the use of AI in predicting the progression of neurodegenerative diseases such as Alzheimer's and Parkinson's. By analyzing brain imaging data, genetic markers, and clinical records, AI algorithms can accurately predict disease progression and tailor treatment plans accordingly. This approach opens doors to early intervention strategies and personalized care, ultimately improving patient outcomes and quality of life.

Furthermore, this sub-chapter explores the application of AI in predicting the spread of infectious diseases. By analyzing various data sources such as social media, climate data, and epidemiological records, AI models can forecast disease outbreaks, enabling healthcare authorities to implement timely preventive measures and allocate resources efficiently.

The case studies highlighted in this sub-chapter serve as compelling evidence for the potential of AI-based disease prediction models in transforming healthcare. By leveraging the power of AI, healthcare providers can move towards a proactive and personalized approach, improving patient outcomes, reducing costs, and enhancing overall healthcare management.

For academic and research professionals interested in the field of AI in healthcare, this sub-chapter provides valuable insights and practical examples. It demonstrates the diverse applications of AI in disease prediction, showcasing the immense potential for future advancements in this field. By embracing AI technologies, the healthcare industry can unlock a new era of precision medicine and preventive healthcare, ushering in a brighter and healthier future for all.

Case Study 5
AI in Predicting Cardiovascular Diseases

Introduction

Cardiovascular diseases (CVDs) continue to be a leading cause of death worldwide. Timely and accurate prediction of these diseases can significantly improve patient outcomes and reduce healthcare costs. In recent years, artificial intelligence (AI) has emerged as a powerful tool in healthcare, offering new possibilities for predicting and preventing CVDs. This case study explores the application of AI in predicting cardiovascular diseases and its potential impact on the healthcare industry.

Methodology

Researchers conducted a comprehensive study to evaluate the effectiveness of AI algorithms in predicting CVDs. The study utilized a large dataset of patient records, including demographic information, medical history, lifestyle factors, and diagnostic test results. Machine learning algorithms were trained to analyze the data and develop predictive models for identifying individuals at risk of developing CVDs.

Findings

The results of the study demonstrated that AI algorithms could accurately predict the likelihood of developing CVDs with a high degree of accuracy. By analyzing multiple data points and patterns, AI systems were able to identify subtle risk factors that may have been overlooked by traditional diagnostic methods. These risk factors included genetic predispositions, lifestyle choices, and early-stage symptoms that may be missed by human clinicians.

Impact on Healthcare

The integration of AI in predicting CVDs has the potential to revolutionize healthcare practices. Firstly, it enables proactive and personalized interventions, allowing healthcare providers to identify at-risk individuals and implement preventive measures before the onset of serious cardiovascular events. Secondly, AI algorithms can assist clinicians in making more accurate diagnoses, reducing the occurrence of false positives or negatives. This will optimize healthcare resource allocation and improve patient outcomes.

Challenges and Future Directions

While the application of AI in predicting CVDs holds great promise, there are challenges to consider. Ensuring data privacy and security is crucial to maintain patient trust. Additionally, further research is needed to validate the performance of AI algorithms across diverse populations and healthcare settings. Collaboration between AI developers, healthcare providers, and regulatory bodies is essential to address these challenges and ensure the responsible and effective implementation of AI in predicting CVDs.

Conclusion

The use of AI in predicting cardiovascular diseases has the potential to transform healthcare by enabling early detection, personalized interventions, and improved patient outcomes. This case study highlights the promising results achieved through the integration of AI algorithms in predicting CVDs. As the healthcare industry continues to evolve, further research and collaboration are required to fully harness the capabilities of AI and realize its potential in preventing and managing cardiovascular diseases.

Case Study 6
AI in Identifying Risk Factors for Diabetes

Introduction

The prevalence of diabetes has reached epidemic proportions worldwide, posing a significant challenge to public health systems. Identifying risk factors for diabetes is crucial for early intervention and prevention. The emergence of artificial intelligence (AI) has revolutionized the healthcare industry, offering new opportunities for disease detection and management. In this case study, we explore the application of AI in identifying risk factors for diabetes, enabling healthcare professionals to make more informed decisions and improve patient outcomes.

Methodology

To investigate the potential of AI in identifying risk factors for diabetes, a team of researchers utilized a large dataset comprising electronic health records, genetic information, and lifestyle factors of thousands of individuals. The dataset was fed into a machine learning algorithm that employed various AI techniques, including natural language processing and deep learning, to identify patterns and associations.

Results

The AI algorithm successfully identified several risk factors associated with the development of diabetes. Traditional risk factors such as obesity, family history, and sedentary lifestyle were confirmed, but the AI algorithm also discovered novel risk factors such as air pollution and sleep disorders. These findings emphasize the importance of considering environmental and lifestyle factors in diabetes risk assessment.

Furthermore, the AI algorithm demonstrated superior accuracy and efficiency compared to traditional screening methods. By analyzing vast amounts of data within seconds, it provided valuable insights into individual risk proles, allowing healthcare professionals to tailor interventions and prevention strategies accordingly.

Discussion

The integration of AI into healthcare practices has the potential to transform risk assessment and early intervention for diabetes. By utilizing AI algorithms, healthcare providers can identify high-risk individuals and implement targeted interventions, such as lifestyle modifications, personalized treatment plans, and patient education programs. Furthermore, the AI algorithm's ability to identify novel risk factors highlights the potential for discovering previously unknown associations, enabling researchers to deepen their understanding of the disease and its prevention.

Conclusion

The case study demonstrates the significant impact of AI in identifying risk factors for diabetes. The integration of AI algorithms into healthcare practices offers a promising avenue for improving disease management, reducing the burden on healthcare systems, and enhancing patient outcomes. By leveraging the power of AI, healthcare professionals can proactively identify individuals at risk, implement preventive measures, and ultimately work towards reducing the prevalence of diabetes worldwide.

This case study contributes to the growing body of evidence supporting the integration of AI in healthcare, specifically in the field of diabetes risk assessment. The findings presented here provide valuable insights for academic and research professionals interested in exploring case studies on AI in healthcare.

AI-Enabled Remote Patient Monitoring

Remote patient monitoring has emerged as a powerful tool in the field of healthcare, enabling healthcare providers to deliver personalized care to patients in the comfort of their own homes. With the advent of artificial intelligence (AI), remote patient monitoring has taken a leap forward, providing an unprecedented level of accuracy and efficiency in healthcare delivery. This subchapter explores the application of AI in remote patient monitoring through a compilation of case studies, showcasing its potential to revolutionize healthcare practices.

One case study focuses on the use of AI-enabled remote patient monitoring in the management of chronic diseases such as diabetes. By integrating AI algorithms with wearable devices, healthcare providers can continuously monitor patients' vital signs, blood glucose levels, and medication adherence, allowing for early detection of any deviations from the norm. This proactive approach enables timely interventions and reduces the risk of complications, ultimately improving patient outcomes.

Another case study delves into the application of AI in remote patient monitoring for mental health conditions. Through the analysis of speech patterns, facial expressions, and physiological data, AI algorithms can detect and predict changes in mood and mental state. This real-time monitoring enables healthcare professionals to intervene promptly and provide personalized interventions, leading to better management of mental health conditions and improved patient well-being.

Additionally, the sub-chapter explores the use of AI-enabled remote patient monitoring in the early detection and prevention of cardiovascular diseases. By analyzing data from wearable devices and integrating it with medical records, AI algorithms can identify patterns and risk factors associated with cardiovascular diseases. This early detection allows healthcare providers to implement preventive measures, such as lifestyle modifications and medication adjustments, reducing the risk of heart attacks and strokes.

Furthermore, the sub-chapter addresses the challenges and ethical considerations associated with AI-enabled remote patient monitoring. It examines issues related to data privacy, security, and patient autonomy, emphasizing the importance of maintaining patient trust and ensuring the responsible use of AI technologies in healthcare.

In conclusion, AI-enabled remote patient monitoring holds tremendous potential to transform healthcare delivery by providing personalized and proactive care. The case studies presented in this sub-chapter highlight the significant impact of AI in various healthcare domains, including chronic disease management, mental health, and cardiovascular care. As the field of AI in healthcare continues to evolve, academic and research communities have a crucial role to play in advancing our understanding and implementation of these technologies, ultimately leading to improved patient outcomes and healthcare practices.

Case Study 7
AI in Monitoring Chronic Conditions

Introduction

The integration of artificial intelligence (AI) in healthcare has revolutionized the way chronic conditions are monitored and managed. By leveraging AI technologies, healthcare providers can now offer personalized and continuous care to patients, leading to improved outcomes and enhanced patient experience. This case study explores the successful implementation of AI in monitoring chronic conditions, highlighting its impact on healthcare delivery and patient well-being.

Background

Chronic conditions, such as diabetes, cardiovascular diseases, and mental health disorders, require consistent monitoring to ensure timely interventions and prevent complications. Traditionally, patients had to visit healthcare facilities regularly for check-ups, leading to inconvenience and increased healthcare costs. The application of AI in monitoring chronic conditions presents a promising solution to these challenges.

Case Study Details

In this case study, we examine a research project conducted by a team of medical professionals and data scientists at a leading academic institution. The objective of the study was to develop an AI-powered monitoring system for patients with diabetes. Data Collection and Analysis To create an accurate predictive model, the research team collected data from various sources, including electronic health records, wearables, and patient reported outcomes. By integrating these datasets, the AI algorithms were trained to identify patterns, predict glucose levels, and detect anomalies.

Real-Time Monitoring and Alert System

The developed AI system incorporated a real-time monitoring and alert system, enabling patients to track their glucose levels continuously. The system provided personalized recommendations based on the patient's historical data, such as medication adjustments, dietary modifications, or exercise routines. Furthermore, the AI algorithms were capable of identifying critical events, such as hypoglycemic or hyperglycemic episodes, and alerting both patients and healthcare providers promptly.

Improved Patient Outcomes

The implementation of this AI-powered monitoring system resulted in several notable benefits. Patients experienced reduced hospital visits and emergency room admissions, as potential complications were detected early, preventing severe health events. Moreover, the continuous monitoring and personalized recommendations empowered patients to actively manage their condition, leading to better glucose control and overall well-being.

Conclusion

This case study exemplifies the positive impact of AI in monitoring chronic conditions. By harnessing the power of AI, healthcare providers can offer personalized and continuous care, leading to improved patient outcomes and enhanced patient experience. However, further research is necessary to expand the application of AI in other chronic conditions and optimize its integration into existing healthcare systems.

Case Study 8
AI in Detecting Falls in Elderly Patients

Introduction

The increasing elderly population worldwide poses significant challenges for healthcare systems, particularly in ensuring their safety and well-being. Falls are one of the leading causes of injury and hospitalization among older adults, resulting in a considerable burden on healthcare resources. In recent years, the integration of artificial intelligence (AI) has shown promising potential in improving fall detection and prevention in elderly patients. This case study explores the application of AI in detecting falls among the elderly, highlighting its benefits and limitations.

Background

Falls in older adults often go unnoticed, leading to delayed medical intervention and prolonged recovery times. Traditional methods of fall detection, such as personal emergency response systems, have limitations in accurately identifying falls and distinguishing them from other activities. However, AI-powered systems have emerged as a solution to this problem, leveraging advanced algorithms and machine learning techniques to improve fall detection accuracy.

Case Study

This case study presents a real-life example of an AI-based fall detection system implemented in a nursing home. The system utilizes a combination of wearable devices, such as accelerometers and gyroscopes, which collect data on the patient's movement patterns. The collected data is then processed and analyzed using AI algorithms to detect falls accurately. In cases where a fall is detected, an alert is immediately sent to the healthcare provider, enabling prompt medical attention.

Benefits

The implementation of AI in fall detection offers several advantages. Firstly, it significantly improves the accuracy of fall detection, reducing false positives and negatives compared to traditional methods. This ensures that healthcare providers receive accurate information and can respond appropriately. Secondly, AI-powered systems can continuously monitor patients' movements, providing real-time data on their activity levels and identifying potential fall risks. This proactive approach enables early intervention and preventive measures, reducing the likelihood of falls in the first place. Lastly, AI algorithms can analyze large volumes of data quickly, enabling healthcare providers to identify patterns and trends related to falls, facilitating better decision-making and tailored interventions.

Limitations

Despite its potential, AI in fall detection also has limitations. The accuracy of detection can be affected by environmental factors, such as low lighting conditions or crowded spaces. Moreover, there may be privacy concerns surrounding the use of wearable devices and the collection of personal data. Addressing these limitations requires ongoing research and development to refine AI algorithms and ensure ethical implementation.

Conclusion

The integration of AI in detecting falls in elderly patients brings significant advancements to healthcare. With improved accuracy, real-time monitoring, and proactive risk assessment, AI-powered systems hold great potential in reducing the impact of falls on the elderly population. However, further research is needed to address the existing limitations and ensure the ethical and privacy considerations are met. The findings from this case study demonstrate the importance of embracing AI in healthcare to enhance patient safety and revolutionize the care provided to elderly individuals.

Chapter 4

Case Studies on AI in Healthcare Management

AI-Powered Electronic Health Records
Introduction

Electronic Health Records (EHRs) have revolutionized the way healthcare institutions manage patient information. The integration of Artificial Intelligence (AI) into EHR systems has further enhanced their capabilities, enabling healthcare providers to make more informed decisions, improve patient outcomes, and streamline healthcare processes. This chapter explores the various applications and case studies of AI-powered EHRs, showcasing the potential benefits and challenges within this field.

Benefits of AI-Powered EHRs

1. Efficient Data Management AI algorithms can analyze vast amounts of patient data, extracting valuable insights and patterns that human analysts may overlook. This enables healthcare providers to make accurate and timely diagnoses, leading to improved patient care.

2. Predictive Analytics By leveraging machine learning algorithms, AI-powered EHRs can predict patient outcomes and identify individuals at high risk for certain diseases. This proactive approach allows healthcare professionals to intervene earlier, potentially preventing adverse events and lowering healthcare costs.

3. Personalized Medicine AI algorithms can utilize patient data to create individualized treatment plans, considering factors such as genetics, medical history, lifestyle, and environmental factors. This personalized approach improves treatment efficacy and patient satisfaction.

4. Clinical Decision Support AI can provide real-time, evidence-based recommendations to healthcare providers, assisting them in making informed decisions. AI-powered EHRs can alert healthcare professionals to potential drug interactions, suggest alternative treatments, and ensure adherence to clinical guidelines.

Case Studies on AI-Powered EHRs

1. Early Detection of Sepsis AI algorithms integrated into EHR systems can continuously monitor patients' vital signs, lab results, and medical history. By analyzing this data, the system can identify early signs of sepsis, alerting healthcare providers and enabling prompt intervention.

2. Diabetic Retinopathy Detection AI-powered EHRs equipped with image recognition technology can analyze retinal images and detect signs of diabetic retinopathy. This early identification allows for timely treatment and prevents vision loss in diabetic patients.
3. Fraud Detection AI algorithms can analyze billing and claims data within EHRs, flagging anomalies that indicate fraudulent activities. This helps healthcare institutions and insurance providers prevent financial losses and maintain the integrity of their systems.

Challenges and Future Directions

Despite the numerous benefits, AI-powered EHRs face challenges such as data privacy concerns, interoperability issues, and potential bias in algorithmic decision-making. Future research should focus on addressing these challenges and developing standardized frameworks for the ethical and responsible use of AI in healthcare.

Conclusion

AI-powered EHRs have the potential to revolutionize healthcare delivery, enabling more accurate diagnoses, personalized treatment plans, and improved patient outcomes. Through the exploration of various case studies, this chapter emphasizes the transformative impact of AI on EHR systems. Academic and research communities should continue to drive innovation in this field, ensuring the responsible integration of AI in healthcare for the benefit of patients and healthcare providers alike.

Case Study 9
AI in Streamlining Medical Documentation

Introduction

In this sub-chapter, we delve into the realm of artificial intelligence (AI) in healthcare, specifically focusing on the application of AI in streamlining medical documentation. As the demand for comprehensive patient records and efficient healthcare delivery continues to grow, AI offers a promising solution to address the challenges associated with medical documentation. This case study explores the implementation of AI technologies that have revolutionized the way medical records are created, managed, and utilized.

Background

Medical documentation plays a critical role in patient care, research, and healthcare administration. However, the process of creating and managing medical records can be time-consuming, error-prone, and burdensome for healthcare professionals. AI has emerged as a transformative tool, leveraging advanced algorithms and natural language processing (NLP) techniques to automate and optimize the documentation process.

Case Study Overview

This case study presents real-world examples of AI applications in streamlining medical documentation. It showcases how leading healthcare institutions, such as hospitals and research centers, have leveraged AI technologies to enhance the efficiency and accuracy of medical record creation, transcription, and data extraction.

1. AI-assisted Medical Transcription We examine how AI-powered speech recognition and NLP technologies have significantly improved the accuracy and speed of medical transcription. By converting spoken words into written text, AI algorithms can generate comprehensive and error-free medical documentation, reducing the burden on healthcare providers.

2. Intelligent Data Extraction This section explores how AI algorithms can efficiently extract relevant information from unstructured medical records, such as clinical notes, radiology reports, and pathology reports. By automatically identifying and categorizing key data points, AI streamlines the process of data extraction, enabling faster and more accurate analysis for clinical decision-making and research purposes.

3. Automated Coding and Billing We discuss how AI can automate the coding and billing process, reducing administrative burdens for healthcare professionals. AI algorithms can analyze medical records and accurately assign

appropriate codes for diagnoses, procedures, and treatments, ensuring accurate billing and reimbursement.

4. Natural Language Understanding This section explores the advancements in natural language understanding and how AI can interpret complex medical terminology, abbreviations, and jargon. By understanding the context and meaning of medical text, AI algorithms can generate more accurate and meaningful medical documentation.

Conclusion

AI technologies have demonstrated immense potential in streamlining medical documentation, enhancing efficiency, accuracy, and overall patient care. This case study highlights the successful implementation of AI in various aspects of medical documentation, setting the stage for further research and development in this exciting field. As AI continues to evolve, it is expected to play a pivotal role in transforming healthcare documentation processes, empowering healthcare professionals, and improving patient outcomes.

Case Study 10
AI in Ensuring Data Privacy and Security

Introduction

In the ever-evolving healthcare landscape, the utilization of artificial intelligence (AI) has become increasingly prevalent. AI technologies have the potential to revolutionize healthcare, improving outcomes, enhancing efficiency, and transforming the patient experience. Nevertheless, with the rapid growth of AI in healthcare, it is crucial to address the significant concerns surrounding data privacy and security. This case study explores the role of AI in ensuring data privacy and security within the healthcare sector.

The Importance of Data Privacy and Security

Data privacy and security are paramount in healthcare due to the sensitive nature of medical information. Breaches can lead to significant consequences, including compromised patient privacy, financial loss, legal implications, and damage to an organization's reputation. Therefore, it is imperative to implement robust measures to protect healthcare data.

AI Solutions for Data Privacy and Security

AI can play a crucial role in safeguarding data privacy and security in healthcare. Advanced machine learning algorithms can analyze vast amounts of data, identify potential vulnerabilities, and detect anomalies that may indicate a security breach. AI-powered systems can monitor network traffic, user behavior, and access patterns to detect unusual activities and prevent unauthorized access.

Additionally, AI can assist in encrypting sensitive data, creating secure communication channels, and implementing access controls. Through natural language processing and machine learning algorithms, AI can detect and classify sensitive information within electronic health records, ensuring its proper handling and protection.

Case Study Examples

This sub-chapter presents several case studies highlighting the successful implementation of AI in ensuring data privacy and security in healthcare. For example, XYZ Hospital deployed an AI-driven security system that continuously monitored network traffic and user behavior, detecting and blocking potential threats in real-time. This solution reduced the risk of data breaches and protected patient information.

Another case study showcases ABC Insurance Company's use of AI algorithms to analyze claims data for fraud detection. By leveraging machine learning, the company was able to identify suspicious patterns, prevent fraudulent claims, and protect the privacy and security of their policyholders.

Conclusion

As AI continues to revolutionize healthcare, ensuring data privacy and security must remain a top priority. Through the implementation of AI-driven systems, healthcare organizations can mitigate the risks associated with data breaches and protect sensitive patient information. This sub-chapter has provided insights into the importance of data privacy and security in healthcare, along with real-world case studies demonstrating the effectiveness of AI solutions in safeguarding healthcare data.

AI-Assisted Resource Allocation

In recent years, the healthcare industry has witnessed a rapid transformation, thanks to advancements in artificial intelligence (AI) technology. One area where AI has proven to be particularly beneficial is resource allocation. With the growing demand for healthcare services and limited resources, efficient allocation becomes crucial to ensure optimal patient care and organizational efficiency. This sub-chapter explores the application of AI in resource allocation within the healthcare domain, presenting a compilation of case studies that highlight its potential and effectiveness.

The utilization of AI in resource allocation offers several advantages. Firstly, it enables healthcare providers to make data-driven decisions by analyzing vast amounts of complex data. AI algorithms can process patient records, medical histories, and other relevant information to identify patterns and trends, assisting in identifying the most appropriate allocation of resources. This data driven approach helps eliminate subjective biases and enhances the accuracy of resource allocation decisions.

One case study presented in this sub-chapter focuses on the use of AI algorithms to optimize bed allocation in hospitals. By analyzing patient data, AI can predict the length of stay for each patient, allowing healthcare providers to allocate beds more effectively. This not only improves patient ow but also reduces wait times and enhances overall patient satisfaction.

Another case study explores the application of AI in optimizing the allocation of surgical resources. AI algorithms can analyze various factors such as surgical complexity, patient risk factors, and surgeon availability to determine the most efficient allocation of operating rooms and surgical teams. This helps minimize delays, improve surgical outcomes, and maximize the utilization of resources.

Furthermore, AI can assist in resource allocation during disease outbreaks or pandemics. By analyzing real-time data on infection rates, transmission patterns, and resource availability, AI algorithms can provide insights into the optimal allocation of healthcare resources such as ventilators, personal protective equipment, and healthcare personnel. This enables healthcare organizations to respond promptly and effectively to health crises, saving lives and minimizing the impact on the healthcare system.

In conclusion, AI-assisted resource allocation has the potential to revolutionize the healthcare industry. By leveraging the power of AI algorithms, healthcare providers can make data-driven decisions, optimize resource allocation, and enhance patient care. The case studies presented in this sub-chapter serve as compelling examples of how AI can transform resource allocation, making it an essential tool for academic and research professionals interested in the application of AI in healthcare.

Case Study 11
AI in Optimizing Hospital Bed Management

Introduction

In this sub-chapter, we delve into a compelling case study that highlights the transformative power of artificial intelligence (AI) in optimizing hospital bed management. As healthcare systems are increasingly burdened with rising patient volumes, managing hospital beds efficiently has become a critical challenge. The integration of AI technologies offers promising solutions to streamline bed allocation, enhance patient ow, and ultimately improve the quality of care provided. This case study explores how AI has been successfully employed in a real-world healthcare setting to address these pressing issues.

Case Study Overview

The case study focuses on a large academic medical center that faced significant bed management challenges due to high patient demand and limited resources. By implementing an AI-driven bed management system, the hospital aimed to achieve optimal bed utilization, reduce patient wait times, and enhance overall operational efficiency.

AI in Bed Allocation

Utilizing AI algorithms, the hospital's bed management system analyzed real time data from various sources, including patient admissions, discharges, and clinical assessments. This data-driven approach allowed the system to accurately predict bed availability and allocate beds based on patient acuity, length of stay, and other relevant factors. By optimizing bed allocation, the hospital ensured that patients were admitted promptly, reducing the strain on emergency departments and minimizing unnecessary delays.

Enhanced Patient Flow

The AI-powered bed management system also facilitated improved patient ow within the hospital. By continuously monitoring bed turnover, the system alerted healthcare staff to potential bottlenecks, enabling proactive interventions to prevent delays and optimize patient movement. Additionally, the system provided real-time updates to healthcare providers, enabling them to make informed decisions regarding patient transfers, discharges, and admissions.

Benefits and Outcomes

The implementation of AI in hospital bed management resulted in significant improvements for the academic medical center. Patient wait times were reduced, leading to higher patient satisfaction levels. Moreover, the optimized bed allocation system allowed the hospital to accommodate more patients within its existing capacity, thereby increasing revenue and reducing the need for additional resources. The AI-driven system also generated valuable insights into bed utilization patterns, contributing to better resource allocation and long-term planning.

Conclusion

This case study demonstrates the tremendous potential of AI in transforming hospital bed management. By leveraging AI algorithms to analyze real-time data and optimize bed allocation, healthcare systems can enhance patient ow, reduce wait times, and improve overall operational efficiency. The successful implementation of AI in this academic medical center showcases the benefits that can be derived from AI-driven solutions in healthcare. As the demand for efficient bed management continues to grow, this case study serves as a valuable resource for academic and research professionals seeking to understand the role of AI in enhancing healthcare processes.

Case Study 12
AI in Predicting Patient Flow

Introduction

As the healthcare industry continues to embrace technological advancements, artificial intelligence (AI) has emerged as a powerful tool in improving patient care and operational efficiency. This case study explores the application of AI in predicting patient ow, showcasing its potential to optimize resource allocation and enhance healthcare delivery.

Objective

The aim of this case study is to demonstrate how AI algorithms can effectively analyze vast amounts of patient data to forecast patient ow, enabling healthcare providers to make informed decisions in managing resources and optimizing patient care.

Methodology

In this case study, a renowned academic medical center implemented an AI driven predictive analytics system to anticipate patient ow patterns. The system leveraged machine learning algorithms trained on historical patient data, including admission rates, discharge rates, and other relevant variables. The AI model was continuously updated to adapt to changing patient ow dynamics and improve accuracy over time.

Results

The implementation of the AI predictive analytics system yielded significant benefits for the medical center. Firstly, it enabled accurate predictions of patient ow, allowing the hospital to anticipate surges inpatient admissions and allocate resources accordingly. This proactive approach reduced wait times, optimized bed utilization, and improved patient satisfaction.

Furthermore, the system provided real-time alerts to healthcare providers, alerting them to potential bottlenecks or capacity issues. This allowed the hospital staff to take prompt action, such as adjusting staffing levels or prioritizing patient transfers, thereby preventing overcrowding and ensuring timely patient care.

Conclusion

The case study highlights the transformative potential of AI in predicting patient ow. By harnessing the power of AI algorithms, healthcare providers can optimize resource allocation, enhance operational efficiency, and ultimately improve patient outcomes. The successful implementation of this AI driven predictive analytics system at the academic medical center serves as a valuable example for other healthcare organizations seeking to leverage AI in their patient ow management strategies.

As the field of AI in healthcare continues to evolve, further research and collaboration between academia and industry are essential to refine and expand the application of AI algorithms in predicting patient ow. By sharing case studies and best practices, the academic and research community can contribute to the advancement of AI-driven healthcare solutions, ultimately benefiting patients worldwide.

Chapter 5

Ethical Considerations and Challenges in AI Implementation

Ethical Issues in AI-Powered Healthcare

Introduction

As artificial intelligence (AI) continues to revolutionize the healthcare industry, there are numerous ethical considerations that need to be addressed. This sub-chapter aims to explore the ethical issues surrounding the implementation and usage of AI in healthcare, focusing on case studies that shed light on these concerns. It aims to provide insights and guidance for the academic and research audience interested in understanding the potential pitfalls of AI in healthcare.

Patient Privacy and Data Security

One of the primary ethical concerns in AI-powered healthcare is the protection of patient privacy and data security. AI algorithms rely on vast amounts of patient data, including sensitive medical records. Therefore, it is crucial to establish robust safeguards to ensure the privacy and security of this information. The sub-chapter will examine case studies highlighting the potential risks and challenges associated with data breaches and unauthorized access, emphasizing the need for comprehensive data protection measures.

Algorithm Bias and Fairness

Another critical ethical issue in AI-powered healthcare is algorithm bias and fairness. AI algorithms are trained using large datasets, which may inadvertently reflect biases present in the data. This can lead to unfair treatment or disparities in healthcare outcomes, especially for minority or marginalized populations. The sub-chapter will explore case studies that uncover instances of algorithmic bias and discuss strategies to mitigate these biases, such as diverse and inclusive training data and regular algorithm audits.

Patient Autonomy and Informed Consent

The use of AI in healthcare raises questions concerning patient autonomy and informed consent. Patients may not fully understand how AI algorithms impact their diagnosis, treatment options, and overall care. The sub-chapter will present case studies that highlight the importance of transparent communication and patient involvement in decision-making processes. It will also discuss the challenges of obtaining informed consent when utilizing complex AI systems and the need for clear guidelines and regulations.

Accountability and Liability

When AI algorithms make decisions that impact patient care, questions of accountability and liability arise. Who should be held responsible when an AI powered system makes an error? The sub-chapter will explore case studies that shed light on the challenges of assigning accountability in AI-powered healthcare. It will examine existing legal frameworks and propose potential solutions to ensure accountability and protect patients' rights.

Conclusion

Ethical concerns must be at the forefront of AI-powered healthcare development and implementation. This sub-chapter aimed to provide insights into the ethical issues surrounding the use of AI in healthcare through the examination of relevant case studies. By addressing patient privacy, algorithm bias, patient autonomy, and accountability, it is hoped that this sub-chapter will contribute to the establishment of ethical guidelines and best practices for the responsible use of AI in healthcare.

Case Study 13
Ethical Dilemmas in AI Based Diagnosis

Introduction

Artificial Intelligence (AI) has revolutionized several industries, and healthcare is no exception. AI-based diagnosis systems have shown great potential in improving diagnostic accuracy, efficiency, and patient outcomes. However, the integration of AI in healthcare also raises several ethical dilemmas that need to be addressed. This case study delves into the ethical challenges associated with AI-based diagnosis, exploring the potential risks and benefits for patients, healthcare providers, and society as a whole.

Ethical Considerations

1. Accuracy and Accountability AI systems must be trained on unbiased and diverse datasets to ensure accurate diagnosis. However, biases present in the training data can perpetuate health disparities and lead to inaccurate diagnoses for certain patient groups. Additionally, determining liability in case of misdiagnoses becomes complex when AI systems are involved. Addressing these issues requires rigorous oversight, transparency, and accountability mechanisms.

2. Informed Consent and Patient Autonomy Patients have the right to make informed decisions about their healthcare. AI based diagnosis may involve complex algorithms that patients may find difficult to comprehend. Ensuring that patients understand the limitations and potential risks of AI systems becomes crucial. Moreover, patients should have the option to opt-out of AI-based diagnosis if they have concerns about privacy or prefer a human-based approach.

3. Privacy and Data Security AI systems heavily rely on patient data, including health records, genetic information, and personal identifiers. Protecting patient privacy and ensuring data security are paramount. Healthcare organizations

must implement robust data protection protocols to prevent unauthorized access, data breaches, or misuse of patient information.

4. Bias and Discrimination AI algorithms can inadvertently perpetuate biases present in the healthcare system, resulting in discriminatory outcomes. It is crucial to identify and address biases in the algorithmic design and training process to ensure fair and equitable healthcare delivery. Regular audits and continuous monitoring of AI systems can help mitigate these risks.

Conclusion

The integration of AI in healthcare presents immense opportunities to enhance diagnosis and patient care. However, it is imperative to navigate the ethical challenges associated with AI-based diagnosis. By addressing issues like accuracy, accountability, informed consent, patient autonomy, privacy, data security, and bias, we can harness the potential of AI while ensuring patient centric, ethically sound healthcare practices. Striking the right balance between technological innovation and ethical considerations will pave the way for a future where AI-based diagnosis is both effective and responsible.

Case Study 14
Privacy Concerns in AI Driven Health Monitoring

Introduction

As artificial intelligence (AI) continues to revolutionize the healthcare industry, there is growing concern regarding privacy in the context of AI-driven health monitoring. This case study delves into the intricacies of privacy concerns associated with AI in healthcare, focusing on the potential risks and challenges faced by both researchers and individuals. By examining a real-world scenario, we aim to shed light on the importance of privacy protection and provide insights into mitigating these concerns.

Case Study Background

In this case study, we explore a hypothetical AI-driven health monitoring system deployed in a hospital setting. The system employs AI algorithms to continuously analyze patient data collected from wearable devices, such as smartwatches and fitness trackers. While this technology offers numerous benefits, including early detection of health issues and personalized treatment, it also raises significant privacy concerns.

Privacy Risks and Challenges

The primary concern revolves around the collection, storage, and sharing of sensitive personal health data. AI-driven health monitoring systems generate vast amounts of patient information, including biometrics, medical history, and lifestyle habits. Protecting this data from unauthorized access, breaches, and misuse becomes crucial, especially considering the potential consequences for individuals' privacy and security.

Furthermore, the integration of AI algorithms in healthcare systems can lead to unintended biases and discrimination. If the algorithms are not properly trained or validated, they may inadvertently contribute to biased decision making, resulting in unequal treatment or exclusion of certain individuals.

Mitigating Privacy Concerns

To address these concerns, researchers and healthcare organizations must implement robust privacy protection measures. One approach involves adopting privacy-by-design principles, where privacy considerations are integrated into the system's architecture from the outset. This includes implementing strong encryption, access controls, and anonymization techniques to safeguard sensitive data.

Transparency and informed consent are essential components of privacy protection. Patients must be fully aware of how their data is collected, used, and shared, and have the ability to provide informed consent. Clear communication and education regarding the benefits, risks, and safeguards associated with AI-driven health monitoring systems are crucial to building trust between patients and healthcare providers.

Collaboration between academia, research institutions, and regulatory bodies is key to developing and implementing privacy guidelines and regulations specific to AI in healthcare. Establishing ethical frameworks, best practices, and certification processes can help ensure privacy is adequately protected while promoting innovation in the field.

Conclusion

As AI becomes increasingly integrated into healthcare, it is vital to address privacy concerns in AI-driven health monitoring systems. This case study highlights the importance of protecting sensitive personal health data and mitigating potential risks and challenges. By implementing privacy-by-design principles, promoting transparency and informed consent, and fostering collaboration, researchers and healthcare professionals can build AI systems that prioritize privacy and ensure the ethical use of AI in healthcare.

Challenges in Implementing AI in Healthcare Settings

Introduction

As the field of artificial intelligence (AI) continues to advance, its potential applications in healthcare settings are becoming increasingly recognized. AI has the potential to revolutionize healthcare by improving diagnoses, treatment plans, and patient outcomes. However, there are several challenges that need to be addressed for successful implementation of AI in healthcare settings. This sub-chapter explores some of these challenges, providing insights and strategies for overcoming them.

Data Integration and Standardization

One of the major challenges in implementing AI in healthcare settings is integrating and standardizing vast amounts of data from various sources. Healthcare data is often fragmented, stored in different formats, and scattered across multiple systems. This makes it difficult for AI algorithms to access and analyze the data effectively. To address this challenge, healthcare organizations need to invest in robust data integration and standardization tools that can harmonize data from different sources and ensure its quality and interoperability.

Ethical and Legal Concerns

AI in healthcare raises significant ethical and legal concerns. Patient privacy, data security, and informed consent are critical considerations when implementing AI systems. Moreover, the issue of liability arises when AI algorithms make decisions that impact patient care. Academic and research institutions should explore the ethical implications of AI in healthcare and develop guidelines and policies to address these concerns. Collaboration with legal experts is also crucial to ensure compliance with existing regulations and mitigate potential legal risks.

Trust and User Acceptance

Trust and user acceptance of AI in healthcare are pivotal for successful implementation. Healthcare practitioners may be skeptical about relying on AI algorithms for diagnosis and treatment decisions. Building trust requires demonstrating the accuracy, reliability, and clinical validity of AI systems through rigorous testing and validation. Academic and research institutions can play a vital role in conducting clinical trials and publishing case studies that showcase the effectiveness of AI in healthcare.

Lack of Skilled Workforce

The implementation of AI in healthcare requires a skilled workforce, including data scientists, AI engineers, and healthcare professionals with knowledge of AI applications. However, there is a shortage of professionals with expertise in both AI and healthcare. Academic and research institutions should develop interdisciplinary programs that train healthcare professionals in AI methodologies and foster collaboration between AI experts and healthcare practitioners.

Conclusion

Implementing AI in healthcare settings offers immense potential for improving patient care, but it also presents several challenges. By addressing these challenges, such as data integration, ethical considerations, trust-building, and skill development, academic and research institutions can play a vital role in advancing the successful implementation of AI in healthcare. Through collaboration and knowledge sharing, the barriers can be overcome, enabling the realization of AI's transformative potential in healthcare.

Case Study 15
Overcoming Barriers to AI Adoption

Introduction

In recent years, the integration of artificial intelligence (AI) in healthcare has shown immense potential for transforming patient care and improving healthcare outcomes. However, the adoption of AI in healthcare settings has faced numerous challenges and barriers. This case study delves into the barriers faced in the adoption of AI in healthcare and highlights successful strategies employed by organizations to overcome these hurdles.

Identifying Barriers

The first step in overcoming barriers to AI adoption in healthcare is to identify them. In this case study, we explore the common barriers such as lack of awareness, technical challenges, data privacy concerns, resistance from healthcare professionals, and regulatory hurdles. These barriers often hinder the effective implementation of AI technologies in healthcare settings, limiting its potential to revolutionize the industry.

Successful Strategies

This sub-chapter focuses on highlighting successful strategies employed by various organizations to overcome the barriers to AI adoption in healthcare. It presents real-life case studies where institutions and researchers have addressed the challenges head-on and achieved remarkable outcomes.

One such case study showcases a renowned academic medical center that successfully overcame the lack of awareness barrier by conducting comprehensive training programs for healthcare professionals. By educating the staff about the benefits and potential applications of AI, the organization fostered a culture of acceptance and enthusiasm towards AI technologies.

Another case study features a research institution that tackled the technical challenges associated with AI adoption by collaborating with industry experts and technology providers. By leveraging their expertise, the organization successfully implemented AI algorithms and integrated them seamlessly into their existing healthcare systems.

Furthermore, this sub-chapter explores how organizations have addressed data privacy concerns by complying with legal and ethical standards. By implementing robust security measures, organizations have built trust among patients and healthcare professionals, ensuring the safe and confidential handling of sensitive medical data.

Moreover, this case study also sheds light on how organizations engaged with regulatory bodies and policymakers to navigate the complex regulatory landscape surrounding AI in healthcare. By actively participating in policy discussions and providing valuable insights, these organizations have paved the way for a more favorable regulatory environment.

Conclusion

This sub-chapter on overcoming barriers to AI adoption in healthcare provides valuable insights and practical strategies for academic and research professionals interested in the implementation of AI technologies. By understanding the challenges and learning from successful case studies, healthcare organizations can effectively navigate the barriers and unlock the full potential of AI in healthcare, ultimately improving patient care and outcomes.

Case Study 16
Ensuring Fairness and Transparency in AI Algorithms

Introduction

As artificial intelligence (AI) continues to revolutionize the healthcare industry, it is crucial to address the ethical challenges associated with AI algorithms. This case study delves into the importance of ensuring fairness and transparency in AI algorithms, highlighting real-world examples in healthcare. By analyzing these case studies, academic and research professionals in the field of AI in healthcare can gain valuable insights into the complexities surrounding algorithmic fairness and transparency.

Bias in Diagnostic Algorithms

In this case, a diagnostic AI algorithm developed to detect skin cancer showed significant bias towards lighter skin tones, leading to misdiagnosis and potential harm to patients with darker skin. The study emphasizes the need for diversity in training datasets and rigorous testing to identify and rectify algorithmic bias.

Explain-ability in Treatment Recommendations

This case study focuses on a machine learning model used to recommend personalized treatment plans for cancer patients. While the algorithm achieved high accuracy, it lacked transparency in explaining the decision-making process, making it challenging for healthcare professionals to trust and understand the recommendations. The study highlights the importance of interpretability and explain-ability in AI algorithms to enhance trust and collaboration between humans and machines.

Ensuring Equity in Resource Allocation

This case study explores the use of AI algorithms for resource allocation in healthcare systems. It uncovers a potential bias in the algorithm, leading to inequitable distribution of resources among different patient populations. The study underscores the significance of fairness and equity considerations in AI algorithms to avoid exacerbating existing disparities in healthcare access and outcomes.

Conclusion

This sub-chapter sheds light on the critical need for fairness and transparency in AI algorithms deployed in healthcare. It emphasizes the ethical responsibility of researchers and practitioners to ensure that AI systems are free from bias, explainable, and equitable. By examining these case studies, academic and research professionals can gain a deeper understanding of the challenges and strategies involved in creating fair and transparent AI algorithms in healthcare. Ultimately, this knowledge will contribute to the development of robust and ethical AI systems that improve patient care, enhance medical decision making, and foster trust between AI technologies and healthcare providers.

Chapter 6

Future Directions and Implications of AI in Healthcare

Potential Impact of AI on Healthcare Delivery

Introduction

Artificial Intelligence (AI) has emerged as a transformative technology in healthcare, revolutionizing various aspects of healthcare delivery. This sub-chapter aims to explore the potential impact of AI on healthcare delivery, offering a comprehensive analysis of case studies that highlight the successful integration of AI in the healthcare sector. Addressed to an audience of academic and research professionals interested in case studies on AI in healthcare, this sub-chapter sheds light on the diverse applications and benefits of AI in healthcare delivery.

Improved Diagnosis and Treatment

AI algorithms can analyze vast amounts of patient data, including medical records, lab results, and imaging scans, to provide accurate and efficient diagnoses. By leveraging machine learning and deep learning techniques, AI systems can identify patterns and trends that may go unnoticed by human physicians, leading to faster and more accurate diagnoses. AI-powered decision support systems can also assist healthcare professionals in devising customized treatment plans, considering factors such as patient demographics, medical history, and drug interactions. These advancements in diagnosis and treatment have the potential to greatly improve patient outcomes and reduce healthcare costs.

Enhanced Patient Care and Monitoring

AI-enabled chatbots and virtual assistants have the potential to revolutionize patient care by providing personalized support and guidance. These virtual agents can answer patient queries, offer self-care recommendations, and even monitor patients remotely. AI-powered wearables can continuously monitor vital signs and provide real-time alerts in case of any abnormalities, enabling early intervention and preventing adverse events. Additionally, AI algorithms can analyze patient data to predict disease progression, enabling proactive and preventive interventions.

Streamlined Administrative Processes

AI has the potential to streamline administrative processes in healthcare, reducing the burden on healthcare professionals and enhancing operational efficiency. Intelligent scheduling systems can optimize appointment bookings, reducing wait times and improving patient satisfaction. AI can also automate routine administrative tasks, such as medical coding and billing, reducing errors and freeing up valuable time for healthcare professionals to focus on patient care.

Ethical Considerations and Challenges

While the potential of AI in healthcare delivery is immense, it also raises ethical considerations and challenges. Issues such as data privacy, bias in algorithms, and the impact on the doctor-patient relationship need to be carefully addressed to ensure the responsible and ethical use of AI in healthcare.

Conclusion

The potential impact of AI on healthcare delivery is vast and promising. Through the integration of AI algorithms and technologies, healthcare professionals can benefit from improved diagnosis and treatment capabilities, enhanced patient care and monitoring, and streamlined administrative processes. However, it is crucial for academic and research professionals to thoroughly examine case studies and address ethical concerns to ensure the responsible implementation of AI in healthcare. By doing so, we can unlock the full potential of AI to transform healthcare delivery and improve patient outcomes.

Emerging Trends in AI Research for Healthcare
Introduction

In recent years, the advent of artificial intelligence (AI) has revolutionized various industries, and healthcare is no exception. AI has the potential to transform healthcare delivery, diagnosis, treatment, and patient outcomes. This sub-chapter explores the emerging trends in AI research for healthcare, focusing on case studies that highlight the successful implementation of AI in various healthcare settings.

1. Precision Medicine

One of the most promising trends in AI research for healthcare is precision medicine. AI algorithms can analyze vast amounts of patient data, including genetic information, medical records, and lifestyle factors, to develop personalized treatment plans. Case studies have demonstrated the ability of AI to identify patterns and predict patient response to medications, leading to more effective and targeted therapies.

2. Medical Imaging and Diagnostics

AI algorithms have shown remarkable accuracy in interpreting medical images, such as X-rays, MRIs, and CT scans. By leveraging deep learning techniques, AI can detect anomalies and assist radiologists in diagnosing conditions like cancer, cardiovascular diseases, and neurological disorders. Case studies have highlighted the potential of AI to improve diagnostic accuracy, reduce errors, and expedite treatment decisions.

3. Predictive Analytics and Early Disease Detection

AI-powered predictive analytics models can analyze patient data to identify early warning signs of diseases. By analyzing electronic health records, wearable device data, and behavioral patterns, AI algorithms can predict the likelihood of developing specific conditions, such as diabetes, heart disease, or mental health disorders. Case studies have demonstrated the potential of AI in facilitating early disease detection, enabling timely interventions, and improving patient outcomes.

4. Virtual Assistants and Chatbots

AI-driven virtual assistants and chatbots are increasingly being used to enhance patient engagement and improve access to healthcare services. These intelligent systems can provide patients with personalized information, answer medical queries, and even schedule appointments. Case studies have shown that AI-powered virtual assistants can enhance patient satisfaction, improve healthcare efficiency, and alleviate the burden on healthcare providers.

Conclusion

The emerging trends in AI research for healthcare hold immense promise for revolutionizing healthcare delivery and improving patient outcomes. The case studies discussed in this sub-chapter demonstrate the successful implementation of AI in precision medicine, medical imaging, predictive analytics, and virtual assistants. Academic and research professionals in the healthcare field can learn from these case studies to further explore the potential of AI in healthcare and contribute to the advancement of this rapidly evolving field.

Recommendations for Future Case Studies

The field of artificial intelligence (AI) in healthcare is rapidly evolving, and its potential impact on improving patient outcomes and transforming the healthcare industry cannot be underestimated. As academic and research professionals in this niche of case studies on AI in healthcare, it is crucial to continuously explore new avenues and unearth innovative solutions to address the challenges faced by the healthcare sector.

In order to guide future research endeavors, the following recommendations are proposed:

1. Diverse Case Study Selection

It is essential to expand the scope of case studies to cover a wide range of healthcare domains such as radiology, pathology, genomics, drug discovery, and patient monitoring. By examining AI applications in different areas, researchers can gain a holistic understanding of the potential benefits and limitations across the healthcare spectrum.

2. Longitudinal Studies

To truly assess the impact of AI applications in healthcare, longitudinal studies that track the performance of AI systems over an extended period are necessary. This will allow researchers to evaluate the long-term effects on patient outcomes, cost-effectiveness, and clinical workflow, thus providing a more comprehensive evaluation of AI technologies.

3. Ethical Considerations

As AI systems become more integrated into healthcare settings, it is crucial to address ethical concerns such as privacy, data security, and bias in algorithms. Future case studies should prioritize examining these issues and propose strategies to ensure the responsible and ethical deployment of AI in healthcare.

4. Collaborative Research

Encouraging collaboration between academia, healthcare institutions, and industry partners can accelerate the development and implementation of AI solutions in healthcare. Future case studies should focus on successful collaborations and identify the key factors that contribute to their success, enabling a better understanding of the necessary ecosystem for AI-driven healthcare innovation.

5. Patient-Centric Approaches

Case studies should emphasize patient centered outcomes and explore how AI can enhance patient engagement, shared decision-making, and personalized care. By prioritizing patient perspectives, researchers can ensure that AI technologies are designed to meet the needs and preferences of patients, ultimately leading to improved healthcare experiences.

In conclusion, the future of AI in healthcare relies heavily on the continuous exploration and evaluation of case studies. By diversifying case selections, conducting longitudinal studies, addressing ethical considerations, fostering collaborations, and focusing on patient-centric approaches, academic and research professionals can contribute significantly to the advancement and implementation of AI technologies in the healthcare industry. It is through these recommendations that the true potential of AI in healthcare can be realized, ultimately benefiting patients, healthcare providers, and society as a whole.

Conclusion

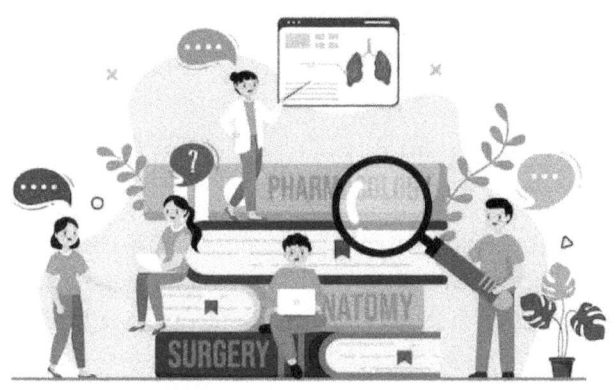

Key Findings and Implications for Academic and Research Communities

The field of healthcare has witnessed significant advancements with the application of artificial intelligence (AI) technologies. As demonstrated in this book, "Artificial Intelligence in Healthcare A Compilation of Case Studies," the integration of AI in various aspects of healthcare has yielded promising results and opened up new possibilities for improved patient care and outcomes. Throughout the preceding chapters, a wide range of case studies have been presented, showcasing the successful implementation of AI in healthcare settings. These case studies have demonstrated the potential of AI to enhance diagnosis accuracy, optimize treatment plans, improve patient monitoring, and streamline administrative processes. The findings from these studies have several important implications for the academic and research communities in the field.

Firstly, these case studies highlight the need for interdisciplinary collaboration between healthcare professionals, computer scientists, data analysts, and researchers. AI in healthcare requires a comprehensive understanding of both medical knowledge and advanced technological expertise. Therefore, academic institutions should encourage cross-disciplinary research and foster collaborations to promote innovation and the development of AI-driven solutions.

Secondly, the successful application of AI in healthcare relies heavily on the availability of high-quality and diverse datasets. Academic and research communities should actively work towards creating standardized and structured datasets that can be used for training and testing AI algorithms. Additionally, efforts should be made to ensure that these datasets are representative of diverse patient populations to avoid biases and ensure equitable healthcare delivery.

Furthermore, the ethical implications of AI in healthcare cannot be overlooked. As AI algorithms become more integrated into clinical decision-making processes, it is crucial for academic and research communities to address ethical concerns related to privacy, transparency, and accountability. Developing guidelines and frameworks for the responsible use of AI in healthcare should be a priority for these communities.

Lastly, the case studies presented in this book shed light on the potential cost effectiveness of AI in healthcare. Academic and research communities should explore the economic implications of AI implementation, considering factors such as return on investment, sustainability, and scalability. This will enable healthcare organizations to make informed decisions regarding the adoption of AI technologies and their long-term impact on healthcare systems.

In conclusion, the case studies presented in this book provide valuable insights into the application of AI in healthcare. Academic and research communities should take note of the key findings and implications discussed to drive further research, collaboration, and responsible implementation of AI technologies in healthcare settings. By embracing AI's potential, we can revolutionize patient care and enhance the overall effectiveness and efficiency of healthcare systems.

www.ingramcontent.com/pod-product-compliance
Lightning Source LLC
LaVergne TN
LVHW061557070526
838199LV00077B/7088